FIRE IN THE KITCHEN

MADELEINE CARDOZO

FIRE IN THE KITCHEN

A MOUTH-WATERING COOKBOOK FOR TEENAGERS

MADELEINE CARDOZO

First published in Great Britain by Madeleine Cardozo.

Mapperton Hill Farm
Mere
Wiltshire
BA12 6LH

info@madeleinecardozo.co.uk

ISBN: 978-0-9566379-2-5

Photography: Madeleine Cardozo
Book design: Jaz Wiseman

Acknowledgements:
I would like to thank all the teenagers and the teenagers to come in our family for inspiring me to create this book.

This book is dedicated to my 6 children, Tilly, Jacko, Lali, Louis, Orlando and Bruno and their 41 first cousins (so far!) Benedict, Elizabeth, Beatrice, Caroline, Felicity, Cosima, Danny, Harry, Barty, Basha, Gigi, Heloïse, Teddy, Freddy, Fabian, Madeleine, Jemima, Archie, Mia, Eliza, Hector, Anastasia, Theodora, Gabriel, Aloysius, Gideon, Otto, Barney, Max, Alessio, Casimir, Tatiana, Maria, Lemoni, Lucy, Rosie, Maggie, Arthur, Florence, Audrey, and Wilbur. Most of them have given me inspiration and some of them have tried and tested my recipes.

Especially Tilly, Jacko, Lali, Louis, Orlando and Bruno Cardozo, Hannah and Oscar Collis, Anastasia and Lucy Irwin, Tatty and Maria Hoogewerf, Jaz and Vicky Wiseman and of course, Damian.

Contents

Introduction

This book is designed to give you as teenagers ideas and ways in which to wangle your way into the kitchen.

Your parents will be delighted – I hope - that you are taking an interest in 'helping' even though it may only be a way to get into the food cupboards legally.

Think of those dreary afternoons when there is nothing to do except wait for the next meal, well with this book you can create the next meal. Everything in this book is easy and when you find it is too easy you can move on to my other more serious books, which involves more time, delicacy and specialised ingredients (not all of them actually).

So when you go shopping or your mother is ordering on the internet, just ask her to add some chocolate chips, condensed milk or marshmallows. They're not sweets they're for cooking with! Some of the recipes here you can make using what should already be in the cupboard.

Just remember the best way to follow a recipe is to **read through the whole thing first**, to see if it is possible given your timescale and to make sure that you have the right ingredients and equipment. There is nothing worse than being dragged off to a dentist appointment half way through making some fudge!

Good luck

P.S Washing up afterwards = Happy, impressed parents

Madeleine Cardozo

CONVERSION

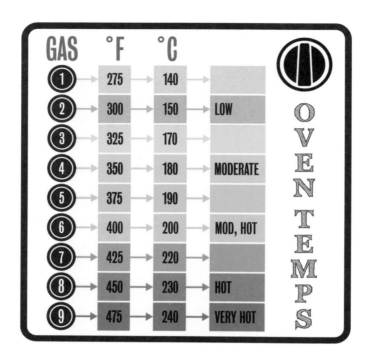

GAS	°F	°C		OVEN TEMPS
1	275	140		
2	300	150	LOW	
3	325	170		
4	350	180	MODERATE	
5	375	190		
6	400	200	MOD, HOT	
7	425	220		
8	450	230	HOT	
9	475	240	VERY HOT	

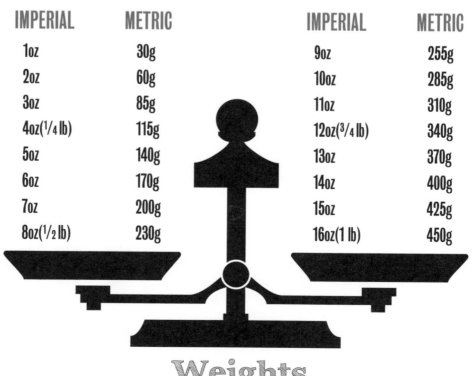

IMPERIAL	METRIC	IMPERIAL	METRIC
1oz	30g	9oz	255g
2oz	60g	10oz	285g
3oz	85g	11oz	310g
4oz (1/4 lb)	115g	12oz (3/4 lb)	340g
5oz	140g	13oz	370g
6oz	170g	14oz	400g
7oz	200g	15oz	425g
8oz (1/2 lb)	230g	16oz (1 lb)	450g

Weights

TABLES

CODE OF SIMPLICITY

 QUICK AND EASY

  TAKES A LITTLE LONGER AND A LITTLE MORE TALENT

   FOR THE ADVENTUROUS COOK

PINT	METRIC	FL OZ
	100ml	3½
	125ml	4½
¼	150ml	5
	200ml	7
	250ml	9
½	275ml	10
	300ml	11
	400ml	14
	500ml	18
1	570ml	20

Liquids

Starters
& Main Dishes

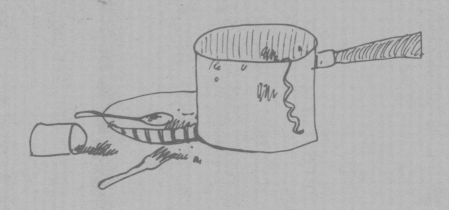

Avocado and Prawns 🍰

Preparation: 10 – 15 minutes   **Serves:** 4 as a starter

This is an all time favourite of mine; I will give you two choices of sauces depending on what you like. This is impressive and delicious.

Ingredients
2 Avocado's
5oz (140g) prawns
A little lettuce for decoration

Vinaigrette
1 tbsp Olive Oil
1 tbsp red wine vinegar
$\frac{1}{2}$ tbsp ordinary mayonnaise
A pinch of salt and pepper

Thousand Island Sauce
2 tbsp tomato ketchup
2 tbsp ordinary mayonnaise

Directions
1. Carefully cut each avocado into half, lengthways down.

2. Take the pip out.

3. Place these 4 halves onto little plates.

4. Get the ingredients for your fillings and mix them together in a bowl.

5. Add the prawns to the filling and then carefully put them into the hollowed out bit of the avocado. You can either be exact and put it in perfectly, but I tend to go for the more relaxed style and let it overflow.

6. Add a few lettuce leaves to the plate for decoration and there you have a delicious starter.

Did you know?
Avocados are not a vegetable but a fruit. Some people, usually in South America, add sugar and milk to it to make a smoothie!

Cheese Omelette

Preparation: 15 minutes   **Cooking time:** 5 minutes   **Serves:** 2

The magic with this omelette is to make it light and fluffy, by whisking it hard. You can eat this with a slice of bacon, a salad or tomato ketchup and mayonnaise. It is yummy, quick and easy.

Ingredients
4 eggs
4oz (110g) cheddar cheese
1 tbsp olive oil
1 tbsp water
A pinch of salt and pepper

Directions
1. Get out a bowl and crack the 4 eggs into it, add the water.

2. Whisk the eggs until fairly frothy.

3. Grate the cheese on the finest grater; whisk this into to the eggs. Add a pinch of salt and pepper.

4. Put a frying pan onto a medium heat, warm up, add the olive oil, spread it around the pan, then add the egg mixture.

5. Cover the pan with some kind of lid, then leave it for 3-5 minutes until the top of the omelette has solidified.

6. Serve with a squirt of tomato ketchup and/or mayonnaise.

Did you know?
In 1987 a piece of cheese over 1,000 years old was unearthed in a Tipperary bog in Ireland. It was still edible! (but, not very nice).

Chicken in Mango Sauce

Preparation: 20 minutes   **Cooking time:** 30 minutes   **Serves:** 4

This is a sweet and sour dish; it is not very hard to do and tastes great. I would recommend eating it with rice or possibly pasta.

Ingredients

1 onion
1 medium garlic clove
2 tbsp olive oil
4 chicken breasts or 4 thighs/legs

6 tbsp mango chutney
5 floz (140ml) double cream
Salt and pepper to taste

Directions

1. Peel and dice the onions and the garlic.

2. In a deep casserole dish or pan, add 1 tbsp olive oil, the garlic and onions. Fry them over a medium heat until they are soft.

3. When the onions and garlic are soft, take them out of the pan, and take the pan off the heat. Don't bother washing it up.

4. Prepare the chicken breasts by cutting each one up into about 10 –15 pieces, if you are using whole thighs or legs just leave them as they are.

5. Get the empty casserole dish or pan, put it on the hob at a high temperature and add the olive oil. When it is hot add the chicken. The idea here is not to cook the meat thoroughly, but to brown the meat on the outsides; this means that the chicken will retain its flavour.

6. Now chuck in the already fried onions and garlic, add the cream and the mango chutney. Give it a good mix. Add a sprinkle of salt and pepper.

7. Reduce the heat and let the mixture simmer very gently for 30 minutes, with a lid on. Stir it occasionally to make sure that it is not burning on the bottom.

Did you know?

When you peel onions a sulphur compound wafts up towards your eyes, this gas reacts with the water in your eyes to form sulphuric acid. Sulphuric acid then stings your eyes, you then produce more tears. To prevent your eyes from stinging, make sure you use a sharp knife as this slices through the cells rather than squashing them.

NEW YORK
BRONX
FAIR MAP
CITY OF
YORK
Compliments
OF
F.W.WOOLWORTH CO.
NEW YO
the
WONDER CIT

Chicken or Prawn Curry

Preparation: 20 minutes   **Cooking time:** 1 hour   **Serves:** 6

There are a few good tricks to making curries and one of them is using the Indian or Thai herbs and spices. Of course you can buy some very good jars of readymade sauces, but making your own is easy and fun.

Ingredients

1 onion
1 medium garlic clove
2 tbsp vegetable oil
2 tsp cumin seeds
1 tbsp medium curry powder
8 floz (225ml) coconut milk (from a tin)

1 lb (450g) chicken breast/frozen prawns
Salt and pepper to taste
Tiny pinch of saffron (the stigmas of a crocus flower, a herb used in many a country and very yellow! Adds to the flavour and aroma.)

Directions

1. Peel and dice the onions and the garlic.

2. In a deep casserole dish or pan, add 1 tbsp of vegetable oil, garlic and onions. Fry them over a medium heat until they are soft. Take the onions out of the pan.

3. If you are doing chicken, cut each chicken breast up into about 10 – 15 pieces.

4. Put the chicken or prawns into the frying pan with 1 tbsp of vegetable oil and fry on a high heat until brown. At this stage you are just browning the meat/prawns not cooking it.

5. Add the onions and garlic to the meat. Add the cumin seeds and the curry powder. Fry gently for a minute or two.

6. Add the coconut milk and the little pinch of saffron.

7. Let all these ingredients simmer for about 45 minutes on a very low heat. Stirring occasionally to make sure that it doesn't stick to the bottom of the pan.

8. Curry's are best if you make them the day before but after 45 minutes it should be delicious too.

9. Eat with some pappadoms and rice.

Did you know?
It's physically impossible for you to lick your elbow.

Chilli Con Carne

Preparation: 20 minutes   **Cooking time:** 1 hour   **Serves:** 6

A favourite and not that hard to do. Go for it, once you do this once you will want to cook it again and again, and people will think you are 'so clever'. If you would like this to be milder/more spicy just alter the amount of chilli that you put in.

Ingredients

2 medium sized onions
1 clove garlic
2 tbsp olive oil
$1/2$ tsp chilli powder

1 tbsp medium curry powder
1 lb (450g) mince meat
1 tin of, chopped tomatoes – approx 400g
1 tin of drained kidney beans – approx 400g

Directions

1. Peel and dice the onions and the garlic.

2. In a deep casserole dish or pan, add the olive oil, garlic and onions. Fry them over a medium heat until they are soft.

3. When the onions and garlic are soft add the chilli and curry powder. Let them fry for about 5 minutes, tossing from time to time.

4. Add the mince meat and cook it for another 5 minutes until it has turned brown, adjust the temperature if it is too hot or cold. Keep stirring from time to time.

5. Add the tomatoes and drained kidney beans add these to the meat and onions.

6. Let this simmer for about $1/2$ an hour – 1 hour, on a very low heat, with a lid on. The longer you leave it the better it tastes. But don't burn it!

7. Add salt and pepper to taste.

8. Chilli con carne can be eaten with baked potatoes, wraps, or rice and a salad.

Did you Know?
Some police forces around the world use a chilli spray as a weapon, it causes a lot of pain. The hottest part of the chilli are the seeds inside.

Eggy Bread - second supper 🍰

Preparation: 5 minutes   **Cooking time:** 3 minutes   **Serves:** 1

This little recipe is so simple and can fill in cavernous bodies when desperately hungry. You can also eat it sweet or sour. Have it as a snack for lunch or for pudding. This recipe is only for 1 person, so you can double, triple or quadruple the quantities depending how many you are.

Ingredients
2 slices of bread
1 large egg
1 tbsp milk
Pinch of salt
Olive oil for greasing the frying pan

Directions
1. Break an egg into a flat dish and beat it with a fork.

2. Add the milk and salt, beat that in too.

3. Get a frying pan and put it on the heat at a hot temperature, with 2 tsp of oil.

4. Place your 1st slice of bread on top of the eggy mix and let the bread soak up the egg mixture. Turn the bread over and repeat.

5. When the bread has soaked up $^1/_2$ the mixture, put the bread into the now hot frying pan.

6. Fry until golden brown.

7. Repeat with the second piece of bread.

8. Best eaten with tomato ketchup and a few slices of crispy bacon.

To make this into sweet eggybread, just add a tablespoon of sugar to your eggy mix, and follow the same instructions. Instead of the ketchup you could use maple syrup.

Did you know?
The average chicken lays about 260 eggs per year and lives for about 6 years, therefore in its lifetime produces on average 1560 eggs.

Fish Cakes 🍰🍰

Preparation and cooking time: 30 minutes   **Serves:** 3 and 4

*This is a very healthy and yummy lunch or supper, I would eat it with a green vegetable such as broccoli.
Otherwise everything else is in the cake!*

Ingredients
8oz,(225g) of any fresh boneless fish – or a tin of tuna, strained
2 medium potatoes
3 tbsp of milk
1oz (25g) butter (a knob)
1 egg
Either fresh parsley or fresh chives
A sprinkle of salt and pepper
1 tbsp Olive oil

Directions
1. Peel the potatoes, cut them into quarters, put them into a pan and boil them for about 15 minutes until they are soft all the way through.

2. Meanwhile get your fish ready by cutting it up into tiny chunks forking it into smaller pieces. Put it into a mixing bowl.

3. Cut up the herbs into tiny bits and add these to the mixing bowl.

4. Add the egg and a little salt and pepper. Mix gently.

5. When the potatoes have cooked strain off the water, add the milk and butter and mash.

6. Next mix the mashed potatoes and the fish mixture together.

7. You should be able to turn these into little cake shaped patties, about the size of the palm of your hand. Make about 10 of them.

8. Into a frying pan pour 1 tbsp of oil and turn the heat to medium/hot. Fry the fishcakes until they are a golden brown. You may have to do two batches.

Did you know?
*Fish is very good for your brain; it contains iodine which is supposed to clarify your thoughts.
Think of those exam results!*

Hamburgers

Preparation: 10 minutes   **Cooking time:** 10 minutes   **Serves:** 6

Homemade hamburgers are an absolute winner, they are healthy and you can add your own touch to your recipe. You can eat them in between two slices of bread or with mashed potatoes and a green vegetable. Here I have laid out the basic ingredients.

Ingredients

1lb (450g) Mince meat
1 onion
1 tsp mixed herbs

$^1/_2$ tsp Salt
$^1/_2$ tsp ground black pepper if you like it
1 tbsp Olive oil

Directions

1. Place the mince meat into a bowl. Sprinkle the herbs and salt and pepper over the meat.

2. Squidge it all in together mixing the herbs in.

3. Divide the meat into six and the make them into flattened rounds. If they are too ball like they will not cook in the centre. Some people like this.

4. Slice the onions into rings or half rings and put them into a frying pan with the olive oil. Place on a low heat.

5. Let the onions gently cook for 3 or 4 minutes.

6. Add the hamburgers to the frying pan and cook on a medium heat for about 2 minutes on each side, until they are a dark brown.

7. Eat quickly whilst hot, or put in a warm oven until you are ready.

Did you Know?
Hamburger's have no ham in them, they are made from beef and that hamburger actually means 'from Hamburg', in Germany.

Houmous or Hummus 🍰

Preparation: 10 – 15 minutes   **Serves:** 6 as a starter with bread

I thought that chick peas were something you found if you split open a bean bag at a school sports day. But no, it has better uses and this houmous is a delicious edible alternative.
Houmous originates from the Middle East, countries such as Turkey, Iran and Egypt, it requires no cooking at all and you can vary it yourself using different spices such as paprika, cumin, chillies...
It is wonderful as a dip with carrots or bits of bread, or it can be used as a spread like mayonnaise to go with potatoes or in a sandwich.

Ingredients

1 400g tin chick peas
1 medium clove of garlic
$^1/_2$ tsp salt
1 tsp medium curry powder (optional)

4 tbsp olive oil – extra virgin is the best tasting
   and most healthy
Juice from $^1/_2$ a lemon – or more if you like it
Parsley or coriander leaves to decorate

Directions

1. Sieve the water out of the chick peas and put them into a food processor.

2. Chop up the clove of garlic and put in the food processor.

3. Turn the processor on for a minute or so. Scape down the sides if necessary.

4. Add the salt, curry powder, olive oil, and lemon juice into the processor and turn on. When the paste looks smoothish, but not too smooth it is ready to scrape into a serving bowl. Add a little leaf or two of parsley or coriander for decoration.

Joke

Sherlock Holmes and Dr Watson go camping and pitch their tent under the stars. During the night, Holmes wakes his companion and says: "Watson, look up at the stars and tell me what you deduce."
Watson says: "I see millions of stars, and even if a few of those have planets it's quite likely there are some planets like Earth, and if there are a few planets like Earth out there, there might also be life."
Holmes replies: "Watson, you idiot. Somebody stole our tent."

Roast Chicken and gravy

Preparation and cooking time: 1 hour 45 minutes   **Serves:** 6 – 8

Cooking a roast chicken is not hard, it needs time and there are only a few things to remember – like to take it out of the oven! The complicated bits are the things that go with the chicken and the fact that you have to time it all so that it is all ready and cooked at the same time. If you do it enough times you soon get used to how it all works. (If you are having roast potatoes, I would start with peeling the potatoes and putting them into a medium heated oven, doused in plenty of vegetable oil – then I would start on the chicken.)

Ingredients
1 medium chicken plucked and gutted – the butcher usually does this for you
Salt and pepper
1 tsp dried Herbs de Provence
1 tbsp olive oil
1 onion

Gravy
1 tbsp plain flour
Juice from the bottom of the chicken dish
$^1/_2$ pint (275ml) water
1 stock cube

Directions
1. Turn the oven on to 180°C 360°F

2. Take the chicken and place it in the centre of a roasting dish large enough so it sits in the middle. Add 1 cup of cold water into the bottom of this – this helps to keep it moist.

3. Cover the chicken with the olive oil, you can use your hands. Sprinkle some salt, pepper and Herbs de Provence evenly over the top of the chicken. Put it in the oven for 45 minutes.

4. Peel and quarter the onion. After 45 minutes add the onion to the chicken dish. Leave for another 45 minutes. This adds to the flavour of the chicken.

5. Take the chicken out of the oven and allow it to cool on a plate for 5 minutes before carving. This will let the chicken solidify a little, making carving easier. Keep any juices left in the dish for the gravy.

6. Now for the gravy. Get a pan, put in any remaining juices from the chicken. There should be at least 1-2 tablespoons of it. If not add a little olive oil.

7. Heat up the juices/oil. When boiling add the flour. Mix very well. Immediately add the water again mixing well over the heat. This should thicken to a gravy consistency.

8. Now add the stock cube stirring all the time so that it doesn't go lumpy or stick to the bottom of the pan. When the cube has melted your gravy is done and can be put into a jug. Taste in case it needs any salt, if so add a pinch or two.

Potato Wedges

Preparation: 5 minutes   **Cooking time:** 45 minutes – 1 hour   **Serves:** 2 as a meal

Now this may seem ridiculously easy, well it is... but the thing is, that sometimes it is good to be reminded that cooking CAN be easy, you don't have to spend hours making something in order to make it taste good. These you can sprinkle with chilli, add grated cheese, eat with a roast or eat them as a snack dipped in mayonaise

Ingredients
6 medium potatoes with their skin on
2, tbls cooking oil
$1/2$ tsp Rock or flaky salt if you have it
1 tsp chopped rosemary

Toppings
a. 4oz (110g) grated cheddar and or mozzarella
b. Sprinkling of chilli powder
c. 1 tsp herbs and 1 clove garlic finely chopped

Directions
1. Turn the oven on to 180°C, 350°F, gas mark 4

2. Wash your potatoes and slice them up into wedges, cutting out any bad bits that you find.

3. Find the right sized oven proof dish, put the potatoes in and then cover them with the cooking oil, get a spoon and turn the potatoes over in the oil making sure that they have all had a covering.

4. Sprinkle your salt and rosemary over the wedges and place into the oven.

5. After $1/2$ hour check them and if you are adding chilli or the herbs do this now. Baste the potatoes – this means get a spoon and collect the oil from the bottom of the dish and spoon over the potatoes.

6. When nicely browned and crispy take out of the oven. If you are adding cheese do this right at the end, then place in the oven for an extra 2 minutes to melt.

Fact
Humans can apparently survive on a diet of just potatoes, and milk or butter, which contain Vitamin A and D, the only vitamins missing from the humble spud.

Quick Chicken Noodle Soup 🍰

Preparation: 5 minutes   **Serves:** 1

An all time favourite for hungry mouths that want instant food, this recipe only takes 5 minutes and is easy peasy.

Ingredients
$1/2$ pint (275ml) boiling water
1 stock cube – chicken flavour
4oz (110g) noodles
Fresh chives – optional

Directions
1. Boil the water in a kettle.

2. Un-wrap the stock cube and put it in a small pan. Add noodles to the pan.

3. When the water has boiled add this, cook for 3-5 minutes on a medium heat.

4. If you would like to add chives gather about 10 lengths of it and cut them up into little pieces. Add these.

5. Pour the soup into a bowl and eat it!

Did you Know?
In China it is a custom to eat very long noodles on your birthday, this is a symbol of long life.

Simple Pizza

Preparation: 20 minutes   **Cooking time:** 12 minutes   **Waiting time:** 40 minutes   **Serves:** 4 – 5

You can never go wrong with pizza. Everyone loves it. This is a very simple recipe and you can put on top whatever is available.

Dough
1lb (450g) bread flour
12floz (300ml) warm water
1 tbsp Olive Oil
1 pinch salt
1 7g packet of bread making yeast
Handful of flour for rolling out

Ideas for Toppings
3 tbsp tomato puree mixed with 1 tbsp olive oil
Onions – very thinly sliced so it can cook
Tomatoes
Bacon, ham, chicken pieces, tuna
Sweet corn, mushrooms or pineapple pieces
Mozzarella and or cheddar

Directions
1. Put all your dough ingredients into a large bowl and mix into a dough. Knead for about 5 minutes and then leave in a warm place like on top of a radiator or in the airing cupboard for 40 minutes to let the dough rise.

2. Prepare your topping ingredients, this means maybe fry up the onions/bacon or get your tin of tuna out and drain it.

3. After the dough has been rising for 30 minutes turn the oven onto 200°F, gas mark 6 or 400°F.

4. Sprinkle a handful of flour onto a flat kitchen surface.

5. Place the dough gently onto the flour so it doesn't stick cut it in half. Roll out the 1st half until it is roughly 20x30cm (the size of a baking tray) and about $^1/_4 - ^1/_2$ cm thick.

6. Do this with the other half of the dough as well.

7. Spread the dough with your tomato puree and olive oil mix as you would jam on toast and then add whichever topping you have chosen.

8. Place in the hot oven for about 10-12 minutes. It doesn't take long!

9. Take out of the oven and transfer to something you can cut on.

Did you know?
The Marguerita Pizza was named after Queen Margherita of Italy. The queen chose it because it was the most similar looking to the Italian flag, Green, white and red: Basil, Mozzarella and Tomato.

Spaghetti Bolognaise

Preparation: 20 minutes   **Cooking time:** 30 minutes or more   **Serves:** 6

Everybody has a different version of bolognaise, now is the time for you to master yours. If I like a particular dish when I go to someone's house, I often ask how they do it. 1) The host is often pleased that you like their dish and 2) you learn stuff. So this is my family version of spag bol.

Ingredients

1 onion, chopped
1 large clove of garlic, chopped
1 tbsp Olive Oil
2 medium carrots, chopped or grated
1lb (450g) minced meat

14oz (400g) tinned chopped tomatoes (1 tin)
2oz (50g) of tomato puree
$^1/_2$ glass of red wine if it is available
Salt and pepper to taste
1 $^1/_2$ tsp dried Herbs de Provence

Directions

1. In a large pan (that has a lid), put the olive oil, chopped onions, chopped garlic and the grated carrots. Do not cover yet.

2. Fry these over a medium heat for about 5-10 minutes, until all the onions have gone soft.

3. Add the minced meat and fry until it has changed from a pinky brown to brown.

4. Add the herbs and a little salt and pepper.

5. Add the tinned tomatoes and the tomato puree.

6. Mix it all together. Add some wine if you have some.

7. Lower the heat; put a lid over the pan and let the whole dish simmer for about $^1/_2$ – 1 hour. Stirring occasionally so as not to let the bolognaise burn on the bottom of the pan.

8. The pasta itself can take anything between 5 minutes and 12 minutes to cook so read the instructions carefully. Always put pasta into already boiling salty water.

Serve with either grated parmesan or cheddar

Joke
What do you call fake spaghetti? An Impasta!

Toad in the Hole & Onion Gravy

Preparation: 20 minutes   **Cooking time:** 15 minutes and 15 – 20 minutes   **Serves:** 5

Toad in the hole is a filling traditional British dish. Everybody likes it and really it is not hard to cook once you know how. Although there are many that are 'not keen' on onions, the way these onions are done brings out the natural sweetness in them. No sugar added!

Toad in the Hole
10 sausages – fat juicy ones
4oz (110g) plain flour
2 small eggs
4floz (110ml) milk
A sprinkle of salt and pepper

Gravy
1 tbsp plain flour
2 small onions
10floz (275ml) stock or 1 stock cube
mixed with 10floz (275ml) boiling water.
Pinch of salt

Directions

1. Turn the oven on to 200°C, 400°F gas mark 6. Put the sausages into a metal roasting tin. Poke each sausage with a sharp knife as this will help the fat escape. Peel and cut the onions into rings or half rings. Put these at one end of the tin. Place the sausages and onions in the oven for 15 minutes.

2. Meanwhile, weigh out the flour and then sieve it into a mixing bowl. Add the eggs, milk, salt and pepper. Beat this mixture starting in the middle working your way slowly to the edge of the bowl. When it is all mixed in you should have a nice thick batter – same kind of mix as for pancakes. Leave it.

3. After 15 minutes take the sausages and onions out of the oven, put the sausages onto a plate and the onions into a saucepan.

4. There should be about 2 tablespoons of oil from the sausages in the roasting tin, if there isn't add some sunflower or vegetable oil. Put it in the oven again for about 1 minute to get really hot.

5. Take the **very** hot roasting tin out of the oven, put it safely onto a surface and then add the batter and then the sausages. Put quickly into the oven and leave them there for another 15-20 minutes.

6. Meanwhile, get your pan with the onions in and add 1 tbsp of plain flour, mix it in.

7. Then add your stock and place over a medium heat, stirring all the time. This should thicken – because of the flour. The gravy is now done. Maybe add a pinch of salt, to bring out the taste.

8. Take the Toad in the Hole out of the oven and serve with something green like broccoli and the onion gravy.

Tomato, Basil & Mozzarella Salad 🍰

Preparation: 15 minutes   **Serves:** 4

This is a very Italian salad, the colours represent the Italian flag! Often used as a starter or a light lunch. It is very simple and utterly delicious especially if you use 'vine' or home grown tomatoes.

Ingredients
12oz (350g) mozzarella cheese
8 medium tomatoes
About 20 – 30 leaves of basil
3 tbsp Olive oil
2 tbsp balsamic vinegar (any vinegar will do but balsamic is nice because it is slightly sweet)
Pinch of salt and pepper

Directions
1. Slice the mozzarella into 1cm, $1/2$" slices.

2. Cut the tomatoes also into the same width slices.

3. Onto either individual plates or one big serving platter lay out the tomatoes and mozzarella alternately, making a pattern.

4. Cut up the basil leaves roughly, place them on top of the cheese and tomatoes.

5. Pour the olive oil and vinegar evenly over everything.

6. Sprinkle a tiny bit of salt and pepper over everything too.

7. This can be eaten with maybe some kind Italian bread.

Did you Know?
Tomatoes are a vegetable, but for various reasons of tax in the 1800's they classed them as a fruit. Tomatoes were first grown commercially only about 200 years ago. Tomato leaves are poisonous and will give you stomach ache if you eat them!

Puddings, Cakes, Biscuits & Sweets

Any flavour you like cake

Preparation: 20 minutes   **Cooking time:** 25 minutes   **Serves:** 8 to go with tea

This is a basic recipe for sponge cake. The wonderful thing about it is that all you have to do is change the smallest thing to make it any flavour you like. You can even mix the flavours such as chocolate and orange or almond and jam.

Basic Sponge

8oz (225g) softend butter
8oz (225g) sugar
4 eggs medium

8oz (225g) self raising flour
$^1/_2$ tsp salt

Icing

3oz (85g) cream cheese
   or soft butter
4oz (110g) icing sugar

Directions

1. Turn the oven on to 180°C, 350°F, Gas mark 4. Grease two 20cm, 8" round baking tins.

2. In a large mixing bowl or electric mixer put the butter and sugar in. Cream the butter and sugar together until they are totally mixed and look pale yellow.

3. Add one egg at a time, beating well after each addition. Add the rest of the flour and the salt. Beat until it is all well mixed in.

4. Add whatever flavour you need at this point. Look at notes below. Mixing until everything has been mixed in. The mixture should be sloppy. Plop it evenly between the two tins and smooth them over.

5. Leave them in the oven for approximately 15-20 minutes. You can tell if a cake is cooked by getting a sharp knife and poking it in the middle, if the knife comes up clean it is done, if it is gooey give it another 5 minutes.

6. Take the cake out and let it cool in its tin for 5 minutes. Next very carefully without breaking it, tip it out of the tin onto a wire cooling rack.

7. For a simple icing put the butter or cream cheese and icing sugar into a bowl and beat until smooth, you can add 1 tbsp boiling water the lesson the thickness slightly. Add whatever flavour you are using.

Variations:
Chocolate: Replace 1oz, 25g of flour with 1oz 25g of cocoa powder, add $^1/_2$ tsp baking powder.
Icing: Add 1 tbsp cocoa powder and 1 tsp boiling water to the icing.
Coffee: Dissolve 4tsp of coffee granules into 2 tbsp of boiling water, add to machine.
Icing: Add 2 tsp of coffee granules and dissolve in 1 tbsp boiling water, add to the icing.
Orange/lemon: Grate the rind of a lemon/orange, add it to the mixture. Add the juices to the icing.
Almond: Replace 4oz of the 8oz of flour with 4oz of ground almonds and 4oz of self raising flour. Add $^1/_2$ tsp of almond essence to the icing.

Banana and Apricot Loaf 🍰🍰

Preparation: 20 minutes   **Cooking time:** 45 minutes   **Serves:** 6 – 8 for tea

This is a little healthier than chocolatey things so if you are feeling hungry for something that is full of eggs, butter, bananas and apricots, this is the thing for you! This is also a good recipe if you want to use up the last of the very ripe bananas.

Ingredients

4oz (110g) butter – soft is best
3oz (75g) sugar
1 tbsp honey
2 large eggs

8oz (225g) plain flour
4oz (110g) dried apricots
3oz (85g) sultanas – optional
3 large ripe bananas

Directions

1. Turn the oven on to 170°C, 325°F, Gas mark 3.

2. Get a loaf tin and grease it. A round tin will do if you haven't got a loaf tin.

3. Put the butter, honey and sugar into a mixer and mix them until they are pale yellow and creamy.

4. Add the eggs 1 at a time let them get really well mixed in before you add the next.

5. Add the flour, mix well.

6. Put the banana's onto a plate and mash them. Chop the apricots into small pieces.

7. Add the dried fruit(s) and the bananas to the mixture, mix well.

8. Put the mixture into the tin and then place it in the oven for 45 minutes.

9. When it is golden brown and you think it is ready, test that the cake is done by getting a clean knife and sticking it into the centre of the cake, if the knife comes out gooey, leave the cake in the oven for another 5 – 10 minutes. If the knife comes out clean it is done.

Did you Know?
Bananas are the No 1 fruit that an athlete eats, it gives an instant energy surge, with natural sugars and carbohydrates. Bananas and honey milkshakes are a cure for hangovers too!

Banana Fritters

Preparation: 10 minutes   **Cooking time:** 5 – 8 minutes   **Serves:** 4

Impressive, easy and deliciously sweet.

Ingredients
4 medium bananas
2oz (50g) butter
3 tbsp golden syrup
Cream or ice cream to accompany the bananas

Directions
1. Slice each banana into three lengthways.

2. In a clean frying pan put the butter and golden syrup. Melt it on a medium heat.

3. When the butter has melted place the banana strips into the frying pan and cook on both sides until they are golden brown.

4. Place three strips onto each plate and serve hot with a dollop of cream or ice cream.

Joke
What did the banana say to the elephant?
Nothing, bananas can't talk.

Banana and Raspberry Smoothie 🍰

Preparation: 10 minutes   **Serves:** 2

Homemade smoothies are incredibly easy to make and you can experiment to find your favourite. Adding a banana is a good secret to a tasty sweet smoothie, also the sugar, evil though it is, brings out the flavour of the fruit.

Ingredients
1 large banana
4oz (110g) fresh raspberries
4 tbsp yoghurt – full fat
1 tbsp sugar
1 tbsp honey
8floz (225ml) milk

Directions
1. For this it is best if you use a liquidiser.

2. Put all the ingredients in together and whizz them up for at least a minute.

3. Pour into 2 large glasses and drink as a pudding or a healthy snack.

Did you Know?
You can make your own ice creams and sorbets as well by making a smoothie and putting it into the deep freeze, after 2 hours take it out, mix it with a fork and then let it freeze again. That's a form of ice cream.

Banoffee Pie

Preparation: 30 – 40 minutes   **Serves:** 8

A success every time! Delicious and not too hard. Sweet and you don't even have to put it into the oven.

Base
4oz (110g) melted butter
8oz (225g) digestive biscuits

Filling
4oz (110g) butter
4oz (110g) soft dark brown
    sugar
12oz (397g) condensed milk

Topping
3 – 4 bananas
12floz (300ml) double cream
2oz (50g) grated chocolate

Directions

1. Make the base first by crushing the biscuits either by putting them into a plastic bag and smashing them into tiny pieces with a rolling pin or by putting them into a liquidiser.

2. Melt the butter, then add it to the biscuits. Mix it together.

3. Press the mixture firmly into the base of a tart tin. Put into the fridge.

4. Now for the filling. In a saucepan melt the butter and the sugar over a low heat, stirring all the time.

5. Add the condensed milk and mix in, stirring all the time, until it starts to boil. Let it boil for about 30 seconds. Take off the heat

6. Pour the condensed milk mixture over the cooled biscuit base Let this chill for about 1 hour.

7. Slice the bananas. Whip the cream gently.

8. Spread the cream and bananas over the top of the pie as beautifully as you can.

9. Lastly grate the chocolate over the top.

Did you Know?
The 'Teddy Bear' was invented in the early 1900's just over 100 years ago. The bears were named after Teddy Roosevelt an American president, who refused to shoot a tethered bear. They then became a craze. Teddy bears also love Banoffee Pie.

Blondies

Preparation: 15 minutes   **Cooking time:** 20 – 25 minutes   **Makes:** About 20 Blondies

This is a very well found secret that should be shared. They are delicious as long as they are slightly under-cooked and gooey.

Ingredients
8oz (225g) melted salted butter
12oz (340g) soft brown sugar
2 large eggs
2 tsp vanilla essence
1 tsp baking powder
$1/4$ tsp bicarbonate of soda
Good pinch of salt
10oz (280g) plain flour
Optional extra: chopped up crystallised ginger, walnuts or white chocolate chips.

Directions
1. Pre-heat the oven to 180°C, 350°F or gas mark 3-4. Lightly butter a 25cm x 25cm or equivalent sized baking tin.

2. Melt the butter in a large saucepan, add the sugar and whisk. You can either put it in a liquidiser or use a hand held electric whisk or a wooden spoon!

3. Let the butter cool down for a minute then add the vanilla and eggs then whisk again.

4. Add the flour, baking powder, bicarbonate of soda, salt, and beat it all together, until a thick creamy mixture. Lastly add any of your optional extras.

5. Put into the baking tin, spread evenly and bake for 15-20 minutes, when you take it out of the oven it should be almost cooked through but not quite.

6. Allow to cool in the tin, then cut into squares.

Did you Know?
Experts say the famous tower at Pisa will lean for at least another 200 years. It may even stay upright well, almost upright forever. That's all thanks to a restoration project, which brought the tower back from the brink of collapse during the 1990's.

Bread and Butter Pudding 🍰

Preparation: 15 minutes   **Cooking time:** 35 – 40 minutes   **Serves:** 6

Another incredibly easy pudding to make and can be altered to make it the way that you like it. You can use normal bread or brioche. Brioche is a sweet French bread, so in my opinion makes a more delicious pudding. You can have either raisins or chocolate chips, the choice is yours, healthy or not so healthy.

Ingredients
10 slices brioche or bread
3 – 4oz (85 – 110g) soft butter
$^3/_4$ pint milk (425ml) milk
2 eggs

4oz (100g) caster sugar
4oz (100g) chocolate chips or raisins
1oz (25g) demerara or granulated sugar to
     sprinkle on top

Directions
1. Turn the oven on to 180°C, 350°F, gas mark 4.

2. Measure out your milk and pour into a bowl. Add the eggs and sugar, beat until the sugar has dissolved.

3. Butter medium sized baking dish all over.

4. With the soft butter, butter each piece of bread or brioche.

5. Spread the bread out artistically over the bottom of the dish.

6. Pour the liquid mixture slowly all over the bread, making sure that all the bread gets moist.

7. Place either the raisins or chocolate chips over the bread, slip some in between the layers.

8. Sprinkle your granulated sugar over the tops of the crusts.

9. Place the dish in the oven for 35 – 40 minutes until golden brown.

10. Eat hot with a helping of fresh cream or vanilla ice cream.

Fact
In France they have an equivalent to bread and butter pudding it is called 'pain perdu' which means 'lost bread'. Traditionally stale bread was used up by making puddings such as these during hard times. Over the years these recipes have changed and become more luxurious, hence the chocolate and brioche!

Gooey Chocolate Brownies 🍰🍰

Preparation: 15 minutes   **Cooking time:** 20 minutes   **Makes:** 10 medium brownies

Chocolate brownies can be made in all sorts of different ways. You can also make blondies, if you don't have any chocolate! These brownies are rich, have no nuts, fudge bits, chocolate chips or chillies added to them, but they are anything but boring.

Ingredients
4oz (110g) butter
8oz (225g) caster sugar
$^1/_4$ tsp vanilla essence
2 eggs
2oz (50g) plain flour
1oz (25g) cocoa powder

Directions
1. Turn the oven on to 170°C, 325°F, gas mark 3. Grease a 20cm square baking tin, put to one side

2. Put the butter, 3 tbsp cold water and the sugar in a large sized saucepan and melt them gently over a low heat. When melted, remove from the heat and let cool for a few minutes.

3. Meanwhile, into a separate bowl sieve the flour and cocoa powder.

4. Back to the butter in the pan, add the vanilla essence and beat.

5. Add the eggs 1 at a time and beat with a wooden spoon or even easier an electric whisk.

6. Add the cocoa powder and the flour and beat.

7. Pour the mixture into the tin and pop it into the preheated oven for 18 – 20 minutes.

8. Take out of the oven and let it cool.

9. When it has cooled, cut the brownies into squares and eat for tea or as a pudding with ice cream.

10. If you want to decorate it put 1 tsp of icing sugar through a sieve over the brownies.

Quote
"Life is like a box of chocolates — you never know what you're going to get."
Forrest Gump in *Forrest Gump*, 1994.

Chocolate Chip Cookies

Preparation: 15 minutes   **Cooking time:** 7 minutes   **Makes:** About 16 cookies

These cookies are quick and easy to do and they only take about 6 – 9 minutes to cook in the oven.

Ingredients
4oz (110g) butter
6oz (175g) light soft brown sugar (granulated sugar if you don't have any)
1 large egg
2 tsp vanilla extract
6oz (175g) plain flour
$1/_2$ tsp baking powder
A pinch of salt
4oz (110g) chocolate chips – or chocolate bar bashed up.

Directions
1. Turn the oven on to 190°C, 375°F, Gas mark 5 (medium sort of heat).

2. Line two flat baking sheets with greaseproof paper or grease the sheets.

3. Melt the butter in a saucepan gently. Do not boil.

4. Put the sugar into a large mixing bowl, add the melted butter and mix in.

5. Crack the egg into a mug, add to the butter and sugar. Beat.

6. Add the vanilla essence. Beat.

7. Sieve in the flour, baking powder and salt. Beat into the mixture – it should be sloppy.

8. Break up the chocolate and pour it into the mixture. Mix in.

9. Take a pudding spoon and spoon medium sized spoonful sizes onto the baking tray. For a tray that is about 20cm x 30cm, 8" x 12", I put 6 spoonfuls on and then pop it into the oven for only 7 minutes or so. Until the edges of the cookies are brown.

Did you know?
It was Christopher Columbus who brought chocolate (the cocoa beans) to Europe in 1502 – 1504 from the 'New World' Central and Southern America.

Flapjacks

Preparation: 10 minutes   **Cooking time:** 10 minutes   **Makes:** About 16 flapjacks

Flapjacks are simple once you know how and you can add all sorts of things to make them more exciting; chocolate chips, raisins, nuts, seeds, blueberries... These flapjacks are great because they are chewy and not too crumbly on the first day and by the second day they are deliciously crunchy.

Ingredients
6oz (175g) butter
4oz (110g) Demerara sugar – you can use any, but this is what I use
1 tbsp golden syrup
6oz (175g) porridge oats
2oz (50g) of a variety of nuts/seeds, I used sesame seeds, pine nuts and sunflower seeds

Directions
1. Turn the oven on to 170°C, 325°F gas mark 3.

2. Put the butter, sugar and golden syrup into a medium sized saucepan.

3. Put it over a low heat and melt the butter. Mix well.

4. When the butter has melted take it off the heat and add the oats, seeds and nuts. Mix it all in.

5. Grease a baking tray that is approximately 20cm x 30cm, 8" x 12".

6. Pour the flapjack mix on and spread around to all the edges of the tray, flatten with a fork.

7. Place it in the oven and cook for only 10 minutes, until they are golden.

8. Take out of the oven, let cool in the tray for 2 minutes and then cut into pieces.

9. Let cool for another 5 minutes and then transfer them onto a serving plate.

Did you know?
'Go.' Is the shortest complete sentence in the English language.

Industrial fudge 🍰🍰🍰

Preparation and cooking time: 45 minutes   **Setting time:** 30 minutes

Once you master this fudge you will have friends for life. This makes an excellent Christmas present for all your relatives, especially grandmothers.

Ingredients

1lb 3oz, (525g) sugar
6floz (175ml) double cream
6floz (175ml) milk
3oz (85g) butter

2 ¹/₂ tbsp golden syrup
¹/₂ tsp vanilla essence
4oz (110g milk chocolate) (Galaxy seems to
  work the best)

Directions

1. Find a flat dish with sides that measures about 20cm x 30cm, 8" x 12". Butter it. Put on the side.

2. Put the milk, cream, butter, sugar and golden syrup into a largish pan and melt over a low heat. You need to stir this occasionally otherwise it will stick to the bottom.

3. When all the sugar has dissolved turn the heat up so that the mixture is boiling. Boil, stirring quite often for about 12-15 minutes. The mixture must bubble.

4. Whilst waiting between stirs, break up the chocolate into small pieces, get your vanilla essence ready and get either a hand whisk or even better electric whisks ready.

5. After 12 minutes drop a few drops of the mixture into a cold glass of water. If the mixture forms a soft ball it is ready. It must not be sticky like toffee or too hard, but something in between.

6. When it is ready take it off the cooker. Quickly and carefully add the chocolate pieces and the vanilla essence. Whisk like mad for about two minutes until the fudge thickens. As soon as it is ready pour it into the flat buttered dish and let it cool for 5 minutes.

7. Whilst it is still warm, cut it up into bite sized pieces.

8. If by bad luck it is sloppy and doesn't set, you will have to pour it back into the pan and reheat it until it does. So get it right the first time.

Did you know?

111,111,111 x 111,111,111 = 12,345,678,987,654,321
12 quadrillion, 345 trillion, 678 billion, 987 million, 654 thousand, 321.

Honeycomb Ice Cream

Preparation and cooking time: 30 minutes   **Setting time:** 3 hours minimum   **Serves:** 6 – 8

This is a very impressive, easy and delicious ice cream but don't eat it all at once otherwise you will be sick. This has been known to happen in my own family.

Ingredients
3 tbsp golden syrup
5 tbsp caster sugar
1 tsp bicarbonate of soda
1 can condensed milk
1 pint (570ml) double/whipping cream

Directions
1. Put the golden syrup and the caster sugar into a medium sized pan over a very low heat. Melt the sugar.

2. When the sugar has melted turn the heat up and boil rapidly for just under 4 minutes.

3. Whilst waiting for that, grease a baking tray.

4. When the 4 minutes are up, take off the heat, add the bicarbonate of soda and beat. This will have a chemical reaction and froth up madly. Pour onto a greased baking tray or some greaseproof paper.

5. Let this cool.

6. In a large bowl whip the cream and then add the condensed milk.

7. When the honeycomb has cooled; smash it up into tiny pieces and add it to the creamy mixture and mix in.

8. Put the ice cream into either a tub or a nice serving bowl and place in the deep freezer for at least 3 hours. It can last for about two months in the freezer.

Did you know?
Refrigerators were invented in the early 1800's, it was only after that date that ice cream was made commercially.

Meringue Baskets

Preparation: 20 minutes   **Cooking time:** 1 hour 15 minutes   **Serves:** 8

Meringues are deliciously sweet and very easy to make once you know how. So here is how.

Ingredients

4 egg whites
8oz (225g) castor sugar
1tbsp cornflour
1 tsp vinegar

12floz (300ml) double cream
8oz (225g) fresh fruit, such as strawberries,
    raspberries, blueberries, apricots, peaches...
2 tbsp chopped hazelnuts or almonds – optional.

Directions

1. Preheat the oven 200°C, 400°F, gas mark 6. Put the egg whites in a large mixing bowl and whisk until the egg whites are stiff, so stiff that they don't change their shape at all.

2. Add ¹/₂ the sugar and keep whisking until it is glossy. 1 tablespoon at a time, add the rest of the sugar beating in between additions until all the sugar has gone and the mixture is firm.

3. Whisk in the cornflour and the vinegar.

4. Line two baking trays with grease proof paper. Onto the paper with a pencil, draw 10 or 12 circles each about 3", 8cm diameter.

5. Spoon the mixture equally onto each circle, make a dip in the middle of each one, making a bowl shape.

7. Turn the heat right down to 130°C, 250°F, Gas mark ¹/₂.

8. Put the trays into the oven and bake for 1 hour and 15 minutes. Turn the oven off, leaving the meringues in the oven until the oven cools down completely.

10. Just before you are ready to serve the meringues whip the cream, spread it into the bowl each meringue. Chop the fruit if it needs chopping and add that onto the top of each meringue.

11. If you have it, if you like it and if you are feeling like a little extra work add a sprinkle of chopped hazelnuts or almonds to the top.

Fact

If your meringues go horribly wrong just crumble up the meringues and mix together with the fruit and cream to make Eton Mess; a pudding invented by Eton school served at their annual cricket match against Harrow.

Milla's Chocolate Biscuit Cake

Preparation: 15 minutes   **Setting time:** 1 hour minimum   **Makes:** About 20

This is a very simple delicious recipe using the minimum ingredients that are easy to get hold of.

Ingredients
7oz (200g) dark chocolate
14oz (400g) digestive biscuits
2oz (50g) cocoa powder
7oz (200g) butter
1 tbsp golden syrup

$^1/_2$ tsp salt
You can add any nuts you like, pistachio's, pine nuts, walnuts, almonds, hazelnuts. This can jazz it up a little.

Directions
1. Find a bowl that will sit comfortably over the top of a saucepan. Quarter fill the saucepan with water. Put the pan on the heat with the bowl on top. This is for melting the chocolate.

2. Into the bowl put the butter chopped up, the golden syrup and the chocolate broken up. As it melts stir it.

3. When it has melted mix the cocoa powder in.

4. Put all the biscuits into a plastic bag and bash them with a rolling pin until they are crumbly.

5. Add the melted chocolate, syrup, butter, cocoa and salt to the biscuits, mix in.

6. Find a flat dish with short sides that you can place this mixture into. Press the mixture firmly in.

7. Let it cool in the fridge for at least 1 hour. Then slice up into friendly sized pieces.

Fact
Cocoa originally came from Mayan and Aztec civilisations in Central America. It was known as the 'food of the Gods'.

Mississippi Mud Pie

Preparation: 1 hour   **Cooking and cooling time:** 3 hours   **Serves:** 6 – 8

I just love the name Mississippi Mud Pie, and this really is quite a porky pudding, delicious and incredibly greedy. This recipe is complicated so follow it carefully. If you can do this successfully you are brilliant.

Pastry
8oz (225g) plain flour
1 ¹/₂ tbsp cocoa powder
5oz (140g) butter
2 tbsp castor sugar
1 – 2 tbsp cold water

Filling
3oz (85g) butter
6oz (175g) brown sugar
2 eggs – lightly beaten
2 tbsp sifted cocoa powder
3oz (85g) plain chocolate
5floz (140ml) single cream

Directions

1. Make the pastry first: Sieve the flour and cocoa powder into a mixing bowl. Rub in the butter until it resembles fine breadcrumbs. Mix the castor sugar in. Add enough **cold** water to make a good dough. Do not over work the pastry.

2. Wrap the dough in cling film and place in the fridge for 15 minutes. You do this to so that the pastry doesn't shrink too much when it cooks.

3. Grease a 9", 23cm diameter pie tin and turn the oven on to 190°C, 375°F, gas mark 5.

4. Sprinkle a handful of flour onto a surface to stop the pastry sticking, roll out the pastry and line the pie dish with it, stab the pastry base all over using a fork.

5. Now you are going to blind bake the pastry. *Blind baking* is the process of *baking* pastry before a filling is added. Cover the pastry with grease proof paper and cover the base of the pastry with either dried pulses (any dried beans or chickpeas) or specific ceramic ones. You use the beans to stop the pastry rising. Place the pastry in the oven for 15 minutes, take off the greaseproof paper and baking beans/marbles and cook for a further 5 minutes.

6. Now for the filling: In a mixer beat together the butter and sugar, then add the eggs little by little. Beat in the cocoa too.

7. Melt the chocolate by putting it into a bowl that sits comfortably over a saucepan that is ¹/₄ filled with water, heat.

8. Add the melted chocolate to the rest of the filling. Add the single cream too.

9. Pour the mixture into the pastry case and cook for a further 35-45 minutes at a lower temperature of 160°C, 325°F, gas mark 3. Take out of the oven and allow to completely cool, this may take a couple of hours. Serve with vanilla ice cream or a dollop of double cream. Evil!

Nutella Ice Cream 🍰

Preparation and cooking time: 15 minutes   **Setting time:** 6 hours minimum   **Serves:** 6 – 8

This is a delicious ice cream. Easy peasy to make. The secret to this is not to add too much Nutella otherwise you won't appreciate it.

Ingredients
14oz, (397g) tin of condensed milk
1 pint (570ml) double/whipping cream
6 oz (175g) Nutella – make sure it is soft but not runny

Directions
1. Whip the cream until it becomes slightly stiff, don't over whip.

2. Add the condensed milk to the cream and fold in gently.

3. Add the Nutella and fold in gently. The idea is not to make the ice cream brown but to have Nutella mouthfuls.

4. Put into either a nice serving dish or into a plastic tupperware box

5. Place in the deep freezer for about 3 hours. Take it out mix it up with a fork and then put it back in the freezer until it is hard. This mixing helps the ice cream not to be so solid.

Fact
During the 2nd World War there was a shortage of cocoa. So an Italian baker called Pietro Ferrero made a paste of hazelnuts and a little bit of the sought after cocoa. Little did he know how popular it would be forever!

Pancakes 🍰

Preparation and cooking time: 20 minutes   **Makes:** About 12 – 15 pancakes

Pancakes for breakfast are such an exciting thing to come down to make on a Saturday morning. Everybody loves them. It is an excuse to be really greedy using all kinds of toppings such as Nutella and banana or maple syrup and cream cheese. Equally you can make an entire meal out of them using toppings such as ham and tomatoes, or pineapple pieces, bacon and cheese.

Ingredients

4oz (110g) plain flour

2 eggs

$^1/_2$ pint (275ml) milk

A pinch of salt

1 tsp vegetable oil

Butter for greasing the frying pan

Directions

1. Measure and put the flour and salt into a mixing bowl. Make a well in the centre of the flour, then break the eggs into it and add the milk and tsp of oil.

2. Get some whiskers – not from the cat but electric ones and starting from the middle; beat the mixture, working your way slowly in circles from the middle out towards the edge of the bowl. The idea is not to get any lumps. The mixture is now called 'batter' should be smooth and thick like double cream.

3. When this is done, get a frying pan, put it on the heat, let it get really hot, (that is the trick to good pancakes) then cut a tiny bit of butter ($^1/_4$ tsp's worth) and swirl the melted butter around the pan.

4. Using a ladle or a small jug pour about 2-3 tbsp of batter into the hot pan. Quickly swirl this around the pan so that the pan's bottom is well covered. As soon as this is cooked, flip the now $^1/_2$ cooked pancake over and let it brown on the second side. .

5. When cooked place on a warm plate and carry on making pancakes until all the batter has been used up.

Here are some ideas about what to put on pancakes:

Sweet – Honey and lemon, maple/golden syrup, chocolate spread and peanut butter, chocolate powder, cream cheese, jam, cream and brown sugar, butter, sugar and cinnamon.

Savoury – Left over bolognaise, fried onions and mushrooms, bacon and egg, tuna and fresh tomatoes, cream cheese and grated cheddar, ham and cheese.

Did you know?

Shrove Tuesday (pancake day) is always 47 days before Easter Sunday. The reason we have this day is because we are supposed to be using up all our luxury foods before a long fast during lent.

Peanut Butter Cupcakes

Preparation: 15 minutes **Cooking time:** 15 minutes **Makes:** 15 large or 24 small cupcakes

Cupcakes are very easy to make, one of the most important parts is taking them out of the oven in time, if you overcook them they will be dry. This is a cheeky recipe as you just chuck all the ingredients in together.

Ingredients
4oz (110g) **very** soft salted butter
4oz (110g) caster sugar (brown is better)
2 medium sized eggs
4oz (110g) self raising flour
2 tbsp crunchy peanut butter
15 – 24 paper cupcake cases

Icing
8oz (225g) icing sugar
1 tbsp cocoa
2 tbsp crunchy peanut butter
3 – 4oz very soft butter

Directions
1. Turn the oven on to 180°C, 350°F, gas mark 4.

2. Put all the cupcake ingredients into a liquidiser or a large bowl and mix together until you have made a creamy dough.

3. Spread your cupcake cases onto a baking tray. Using a spoon, spoon the dough into the cupcake cases until each one is $^3/_4$ full.

4. Place in the oven for approximately 15 minutes

5. While the cakes are cooking; put the icing sugar, cocoa powder, peanut butter and the butter into the liquidiser or a large mixing bowl and mix until a paste is created. Keep this soft, by not letting it get too cold. If it is not sloppy enough add a **little** bit of boiling water.

6. Do the cake test, by taking a clean sharp knife and dip it into one of the cakes, if it comes out smooth the cakes are cooked.

7. Take the cakes out, take off the baking tray and cool on a wire rack.

8. When cold, spread the icing decoratively on the top of each cake.

Did you know?
The sun is so large that 1.3 million earths can fit inside it.

Peppermint Creams

Preparation time: 20 – 30 minutes   **Makes:** About 30

Very easy to make, everyone loves them and they make extremely good Christmas presents too. They will keep for about 1 week, after that they get a bit nasty. This recipe is versatile you can use peppermint flavouring, rosewater, violet, orange essence... In this recipe I have also coated them with chocolate which adds to the professionalism of the creams. You could even sell them!

Ingredients
8oz (225g) icing sugar
3 tbsp condensed milk
A few drops of your chosen flavouring

A few drops of your chosen colouring
4oz (110g) any chocolate you like – plain is good

Directions
1. Sieve the icing sugar into a large bowl.

2. Add the condensed milk, flavouring and colouring. The colouring is very powerful so add only a few drops, you can always add more later.

3. Mix it all together, to make a dough ball, you may need to add a little more condensed milk or icing sugar. The ball must not be sticky!

4. At this point taste it to see if you have added enough flavouring.

5. Get a plate and sieve a fine coating of icing sugar onto it.

6. Make whatever shapes you like, use icing sugar to stop the stickiness. Place them on the plate and then into the fridge.

7. Get a pan and fill it $1/4$ with water. Over the pan place a bowl that sits well. Put the chocolate into the bowl. Put the pan over the heat and melt the chocolate.

8. Dip the creams into the chocolate, put back onto the plate and into the fridge. These creams are best eaten after they have set properly – a few hours.

Did you know?
Eating peppermints after dinner helps with digestion, the oils in the mint relax the muscles of your intestines. Nice hey?

Stickyfied Goo

Preparation time: 25 – 30 minutes   **Serves:** 8 for tea

This is a wonderful party cake, it is very light and once made it is very un messy. The idea is to just chuck all the ingredients in and hope for the best. So here goes.

Ingredients
8oz (225g) marshmallows
8oz (225g) toffees
4oz (110g) butter
8oz (225g) rice crispies

Directions
1. Get a cake tin that measure about 20cm, 8" wide and at least 10cm, 4" deep and grease it. You can actually make this cake any size or shape that you want as you will mould it rather than cook it.

2. In a very large pan place all the toffees, marshmallow and butter.

3. Put this on a low heat and melt it all together. Mixing all the time so that it doesn't burn on the bottom.

4. When it has all melted add the rice crispies. Mix these in well.

5. Pour the mixture into the tin and squish it into all the corners.

6. Let this set in the fridge for at least 1 hour before serving.

7. You can decorate it with all sorts of yummy sweets; it makes a great birthday cake.

Riddle
What do the dead eat, but if the living eat it they die?

St Louis Chocolate Cake

Preparation: 25 minutes   **Cooking time:** 35 minutes   **Serves:** 8 – 10 for tea

There are a lot of St Louis'; this one is famous for his chocolate cake! Although I don't think that he has been made a saint by the Pope himself. This is a squidgy, moist, chocolatey success, and exceedingly rich.

Ingredients
8oz (225g) plain chocolate
6oz (175g) unsalted butter
8oz (225g) castor sugar

4oz (110g) plain flour
6 egg yolks
6 egg whites

Topping
8oz (225g) plain chocolate
8floz (225ml) double cream

Directions

1. Turn the oven on to 180°C, 350°F, gas mark 4. Get a 20cm, 8" diameter cake tin and grease it well.

2. Find a bowl that will sit comfortably over the top of a saucepan. Quarter fill the saucepan with water. Put the pan on the heat with the bowl on top. Break the chocolate up and put it into this bowl for melting.

3. Add the butter to the chocolate and melt this too, mix it gently. Take it off the heat and let it cool.

4. Mix the egg yolks with the sugar. Add the flour, butter, sugar and egg yolks to the chocolate mixture and mix it all together.

5. In a separate large bowl get the egg whites and beat them with an electric whisker, until they are stiff like mountain peaks.

6. Carefully add the chocolate mixture to the egg whites and fold in. Do not beat as this will take the airiness out. Put it in the greased cake tin and then into the oven.

7. After 35 minutes take the cake out. It may not seem done but it will set as it cools. Let the cake cool in the tin.

8. Meanwhile as before melt the chocolate in a bowl over a saucepan with water in, add the cream and mix together. Allow to cool a little.

9. When the cake has cooled turn it upside down onto plate, pour the topping on top and spread carefully. Add any kind of decoration you like, but you won't need much.

Did you know?
Maturing brains need sleep. Babies sleep for about 16 – 18 hours a day, children and teenagers need at least 10 hours a night. Old people need the least, about 6 hours per night.

Write your favourite recipes here

Write your favourite recipes here

Write your favourite recipes here

Write your favourite recipes here

Index